Word Whirls

and other shape poems

Word Whirls

and other shape poems

Collected By

JOHN FOSTER

OXFORD
UNIVERSITY PRESS

Illustrations by *Clare Hemstock*
Cover Design by *Bottle and Co*

OXFORD
UNIVERSITY PRESS

Great Clarendon Street, Oxford OX2 6DP

Oxford University Press is a department of the University of Oxford.
It furthers the University's objective of excellence in research, scholarship,
and education by publishing worldwide in

Oxford New York

Athens Auckland Bangkok Bogotá Buenos Aires Calcutta
Cape Town Chennai Dar es Salaam Delhi Florence Hong Kong Istanbul
Karachi Kuala Lumpur Madrid Melbourne Mexico City Mumbai
Nairobi Paris São Paulo Shanghai Singapore Taipei Tokyo Toronto Warsaw

with associated companies in Berlin Ibadan

Oxford is a registered trade mark of Oxford University Press
in the UK and in certain other countries

British Library Cataloguing in Publication Data available

ISBN 0 19 276189 7 (hardback)
ISBN 0 19 276188 9 (paperback)

Printed in China

Contents

Word Whirls   *John Foster*   8

Wrinkled Snarls and Paddle Paws

Tall Talk	*J. Patrick Lewis*	10
Snake's Dance	*Dave Calder*	11
Lion	*Julie Holder*	12
Hippopotamus	*Julie Holder*	13
Frog	*Jenny Morris*	14
Spider	*Trevor Millum*	15
Doggerel	*Jenny Morris*	15
Mined By Moles	*Gina Douthwaite*	16
Cat Dream	*Catherine Benson*	18
Blackbird	*Gina Douthwaite*	19
Invasion	*Pamela Gillilan*	20
Alphabirds	*Dave Calder*	21

Sunshape, Skyscape

Sunrise	*Mike Johnson*	23
Trees	*Julie Holder*	24
Umbrella	*Catherine Benson*	25
Autumn	*Tony Langham*	26
Fire	*Julie Holder*	27
Winter	*J. Patrick Lewis*	28
Winter Walk	*Patricia Leighton*	29
Holiday Memories	*Paula Edwards*	30
Snowdrop	*Helena Hinn*	31
Listen	*Maggie Holmes*	32
Seahorses	*Janis Priestley*	33
Stone Haiku	*Michael Harrison*	34

Food for Thought

Breakfast	*Noel Petty*	36
Sisters	*Gina Douthwaite*	37
Mirror	*J. Patrick Lewis*	38
Catherine Wheel	*David Horner*	39
Eating Out	*Judith Nicholls*	40
Candy Bar	*Robert Froman*	42
Spaghetti Poem	*Sue Cowling*	43
Orange	*John Cotton*	44
Pineapple	*John Cotton*	45
Drink Me!	*Mike Johnson*	46
Filtered Magic	*Trevor Harvey*	47

Beware the Allivator

The Allivator	*Roger McGough*	49
The Claw	*Dave Calder*	50
Creature	*Dave Calder*	51
Nessie	*Judith Nicholls*	52
Corn Circle	*Pam Gidney*	53
Save the Smorkle Campaign	*Sue Cowling*	54
The Twenty Steps to the Cellar	*Wes Magee*	55
For Sale	*Gina Douthwaite*	56
Hallowe'en Hot-Pot	*Gina Douthwaite*	57

Word Smattering

Word Smattering	*Sue Cowling*	59
Dizzy Dancer's Disco Party Invitation	*Gina Douthwaite*	60
The Letter That Was Never Sent	*Trevor Millum*	61
Rhythm Machine	*Trevor Harvey*	62
I Am The Phone	*Trevor Millum*	64
Music	*David Poulter*	64

Fun and Games

Dive and Dip	*Max Fatchen*	66
Football	*Katherine Gallagher*	67
How To Line Up Your Team	*John Coldwell*	68
Duck	*John Coldwell*	71
Cricket Bat	*Jenny Morris*	72
Such a Racket	*Max Fatchen*	73
Playtime	*David Horner*	74
Only a Game	*Steve Bowkett*	75
When You Walked Down the Passage	*Trevor Millum*	76

From Top to Toe

Bodies	*Gina Douthwaite*	78
Riddle Poem	*Trevor Millum*	79
I Need Contact Lenses	*John Hegley*	80
Blow This	*Gina Douthwaite*	81
Belt	*John Foster*	82
Pants	*Dave Calder*	83
Shoe	*Trevor Millum*	84

Steel, Stone, and Concrete

Pylons	*Christine Morton*	86
Skyscrapers	*Tony Langham*	87
The Bridge	*Andrew Collett*	88
Pyramid	*Dave Calder*	89
Weekend in the Country	*Robert Froman*	90
The Concrete Poem	*Noel Petty*	91
Index of titles and first lines		92
Index of authors		94
Acknowledgements		95

Word Whirls

On the wheel of words, words whirl, words swirl, words twist, words twirl.

Inside the wheel of words, words dance, words prance, words spin, words grin.

Words curl, words whirl.

John Foster

Wrinkled Snarls
and
Paddle Paws

Tall Talk

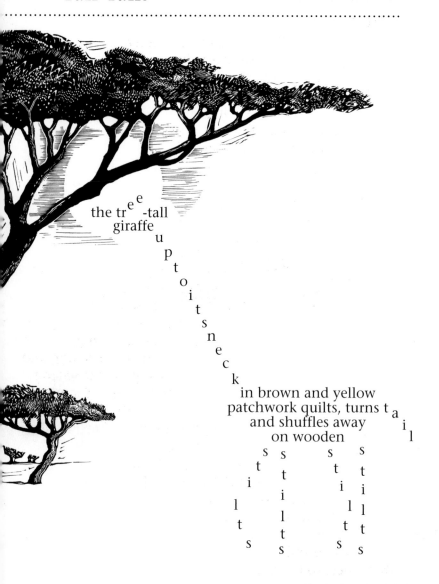

the tr^e^e^-tall
giraffe
u
p
t
o
i
t
s
n
e
c
k
in brown and yellow
patchwork quilts, turns t a
and shuffles away   i
on wooden   l

s   s   s   s
t   s   t   s
i   t   i   t
          i   i
l   l   l   l
t   t   t
s   s   s   s

J. Patrick Lewis

10

Snake's Dance

Sensuous slither
slinkiest slide
the slip in the silence
the hiss and glide
steadily sweeping
shuddering squirm
quivering question
conquering worm
I start sliding this side,
certain and sure.
I spiral all scaly,
coiling a tower,
twisting and toiling,
spellbound by stealth,
I slip through the circle
and surprise myself.
Head is for seeing,
tail is for squeezing,
tongue is for telling and
fangs are for seizing;
stretching and spinning
I sway to the song—
I go as I must,
as I must go on
Sudden is speed like
a wave of the sea,
swift is the sense
as wind in tall trees,
strong is as subtle
as wise is indeed,
they kneel to no one
who're born without knees . . .

Dave Calder

Lion

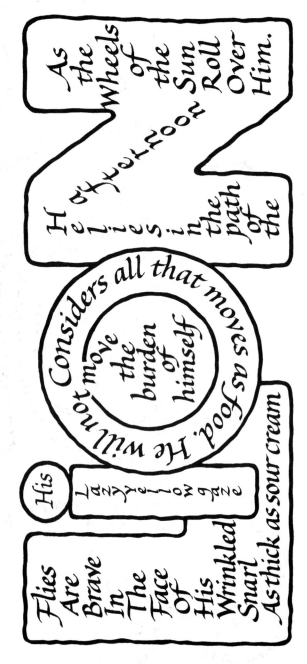

Julie Holder

As the wheels of the Sun Roll Over Him.

He lies in the path of the

Considers all that move as food. He will not move the burden of himself

His

Lazy Yellow gaze

Flies Are Brave In The Face Of His Wrinkled Snarl As thick as sour cream

Hippopotamus

If you sat on a Hippo would it slop about like a water bed would it wobble like a water-filled balloon? Would it feel sticky like a jelly if you stroked it? Would it dent like a water-logged sponge if you poked it? When they open mouths that wide does the river rush inside like a whirlpool? Together Hippos wallow like submarines with legs. They eat like horses and make noises in the water like giant whoopee cushions. They moo like Hippopotatoes in a stew. They fight like battleships. They dance on river beds like cannons booming. When they open mouths would it splash? If you smacked it would it burst if it crashed?

Julie Holder

13

UGLY SISTERS MAKE YOU WINCE. THERE WAS A HANDSOME PRINCE THAT GIRL UNTIL GAVE ME A KISS AND CAUSED THIS METAMORPHOSIS

Jenny Morris

Spider

trapping flies
a thousand eggs
SPIDER
Spying eyes
Spindle legs
SPIDER!

Trevor Millum

Doggerel

"WHAT A DOG?" MEANS UGLY." "WHAT A BITCH!" IS SPITEFUL. BUT WE DOGS BARK SMUGLY. FOR WHEN A CANINE'S FRIGHTFUL WE THINK "WHAT A PERSON!" AS OUR VERSION. DEROGATORY IS SPITEFUL.

Jenny Morris

15

Mined by Moles

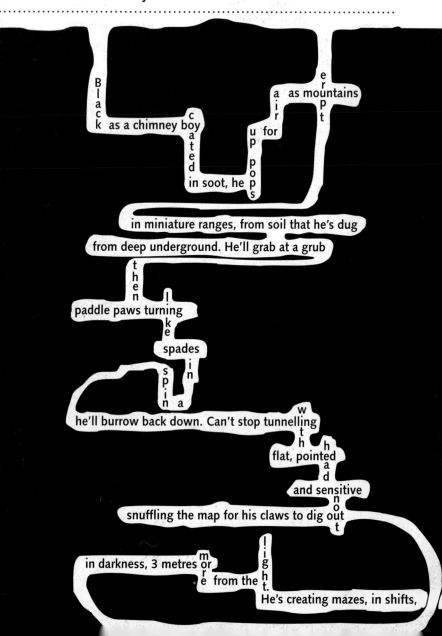

Black as a chimney boy coated in soot, he up pops for air erupt as mountains in miniature ranges, from soil that he's dug from deep underground. He'll grab at a grub then paddle paws turning like spades in a spin he'll burrow back down. Can't stop tunnelling with flat, pointed head and sensitive not snuffling the map for his claws to dig out in darkness, 3 metres or more from the light. He's creating mazes, in shifts,

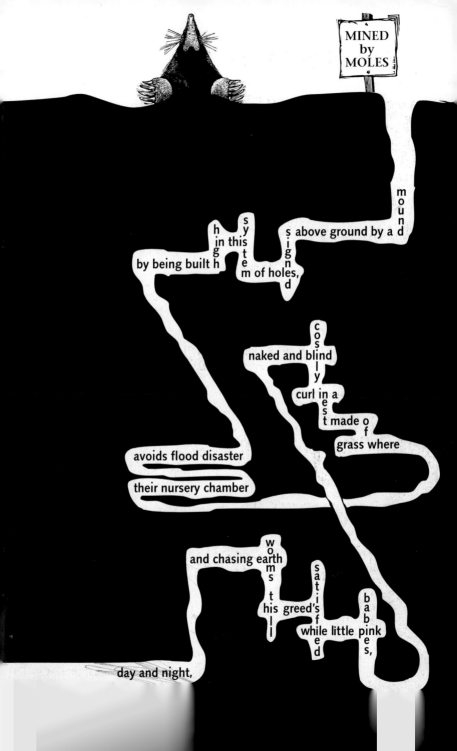

MINED
by
MOLES

mound

above ground by a

sign

in this

system

of holes,

by being built high

naked and blind

cosily

curl in a nest made of

grass where

avoids flood disaster

their nursery chamber

and chasing earth

worms till

his greed's

satisfied

babes,

while little pink

day and night,

Cat Dream

Catherine Benson

Blackbird

Bl^{ac}k
🐦 bird.
Dead.
Dumped
in a bin. Your
life has been
taken. It seems
such a sin.
Did you fly at
a window that
mirrored the
tree? Not
everything
is what
it's
seen
to be.

Gina Douthwaite

Invasion

WITH THE FIRST EDGE OF LIGHT
THE GULLS CAME BEATING IN
FROM THE SEA
OVER

THE FARMLAND INTO ROOFCOUNTRY. DUST-
BIN COUNTRY, WAKING THE
TOWN

FROM ITS SUNDAY MORNING BED. THEY
FILLED THE AIR WITH THE
SCREAMS

OF THEIR DISSENSION, FILLED THE PALE
SKY WITH THEIR ARROGANT
STRONG

WINGS. WHEELING AND WEAVING THEY BUILT
A TOWERING PATTERN OF FLIGHT
ABOVE THE
TOWN.

Pamela Gillilan

Alphabirds

Ys owl

```
    YYY
    YYY
 YYYYYYY
 YYYYYYY
 Y YYY Y
   Y  Y
```

Cgull

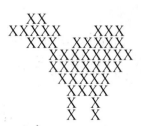

```
    cc          ccc
 c     c   cc
      ccc
```

Pcock

```
    pppp
   ppppp p
 pppppppppp
ppppppppppp
    pppp
    pp
```

Chicken wire

```
   XX
 XXXXX        XXX
 XXX   XXXXX
       XXXXXXXX X
       XXXXXXX
       XXXXX
       XXXX
       X  X
       X  X
```

Dave Calder

Sunshape,
Skyscape

horiz   n

horiz$O$n

horiz$O$n

O
horiz   n

Mike Johnson

Trees

Julie Holder

Umbrella

Catherine Benson

Autumn

SLOWLY SLOWLY THE LEAVES START TO FALL LOOKS LIKE AUTUMN'S DECIDED TO PAY US A CALL

26

Tony Langham

Fire

....

FIRE
THAT WAVES THE FLAG OF
THE QUIET GHOST OF SMOKE
HIGHER
FURTHER
SPREADS
OF SMOKE
A WISP
THEN THE FLAMES
THAT LICK A HOLE
IN THE DARK
SPARK
THE
THEN
FIRST THE KINDLING

Julie Holder

27

Winter

When sky unravels its cold myst-eries fluttering down brown skeletons of trees barely show speckles on a page can these the spectacle of un-expected snow

J. Patrick Lewis

Winter Walk

go.
to
like
would
we
where
show
snow
the
in
Footsteps

Patricia Leighton

Holiday Memories

IT WAS  COLD

AND I WAS FEELING REALY *FED UP*

AND  TO THE SKIN!

I REMEMBERED THE *FANTASTIC* HOLIDAY IN SPAIN—

 HOT WEATHER, CLEAR BLUE SEA,

BOILING BEACHES AND A CLEAR SKY.

NOW IT'S ALL A MEMORY.

Paula Edwards

Snowdrop

a thread of light in the darkness

a flicker of flame in the night

a single snowdrop shooting up from the earth

anticipating spring to come

Helena Hinn

Listen

Hear the spatter
of the rain
Beat a rhythm
on the pane

Sending ripples through the puddles

Water rushing like a stream

Hear the anger of the rivers

Gushing torrents with a scream

As the motions of the oceans

Tremble, raging through the seas.

Maggie Holmes

Seahorses

Waves
and breakers
tumbling, ✱ rippling
across the sea,
smash them-
selves to
pieces, on
the shore,
in front of me.
When angry tempests
blow, wild horses
out of reach, plunge   and
toss snowy heads   and race
towards the beach.   White
crested seahorses,
prancing towards
the land. Each
striving to
be first to
collapse
upon the
strand.
Seahor-
Janis Priestley   ses,
sea-
hor-
ses,
white
breakers
on the
sand.

33

Ground by cold rolling sea to smoothness, I fit now into your warm hand.

Hold me in your hand so your warmth can seep slowly into my cold heart.

Paper is flighty, But my calm gravity will keep it down to earth.

Put your ear to me: what will be ready to hatch if I crack open?

Michael Harrison

Food for
Thought

Breakfast

My daddy reads at breakfast,
We sometimes hear a mutter,
We wonder what he's up to
It must be fascinating, but
If one of us should ask him,
But Mummy says it's cricket,
Then when he folds his paper
His egg and toast are eaten,
So, when I need permission
I don't ask him at teatime
I wait until it's breakfast,
And if he mumbles 'Mmmm',

He holds THE TIMES up high.
And sometimes catch a sigh.
Behind that screen of print.
We've not the smallest hint.
He says it's 'world affairs',
Or boring stocks and shares.
And grabs his things to go,
Quite how, we'll never know.
For something I have planned,
—For then he'd understand—
Then make my special plea,
That's good enough for me!

Noel Petty

Sisters

ssssssisssssssterssssss ssssssssssisssssssterssssssssss

Gina Douthwaite

Mirror rorriM

You looking out	tuo gnikool uoY
at me looking in—	—ni gnikool em ta
I am an **I**-	-**I** na ma I
dentical twin!	!niwt lacitned
Did I just wink?	?kniw tsuj I diD
I thought I did,	,did I thguoht I
because you flut-	-tulf uoy esuaceb
tered your eyelid.	.dileye ruoy deret
When one of you	uoy fo eno nehW
makes two of me	em fo owt sekam
there's twice as much	hcum sa eciwt s'ereht
of *us* to see!	!ees ot *su* fo

J. Patrick Lewis

38

Catherine Wheel

David Horner

Eating Out

Lean cuisine
is not my scene...

FAT CUISINE
CREAM CUISINE,
GREASY-SPOON-CANTEEN CUISINE
DON'T-SERVE-A-SPRAT
JUST-SERVE-A-SPRAT
CUISINE
TRIPLE-PORTION BEAN
CUISINE...
NEVER MIND
YOUR MEAN CUISINE
TRIFLE WITH ICE CREAM
CUISINE
IS SOMETHING MORE LIKE
<u>MY</u> CUISINE!

Judith Nicholls

41

Candy Bar

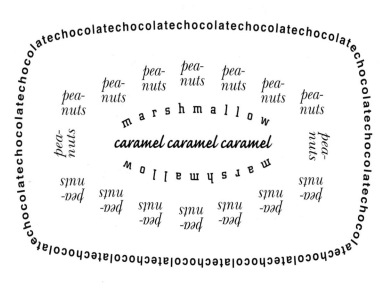

Too much.
Too much.
But I'll have one more.

Robert Froman

Spaghetti Poem

Forks are for twirling s p a g h e t t i

But sometimes it slips straight t h r o u g h

If you find a strand t r a i l i n g

Suck s l o w l y — or failing

That, nip it in ha lf as you chew s p a g h e t t i

Sue Cowling

Orange

I am a bright round orange

Quite sun-like in my beauty,

Peel off my skin
        and then you'll find

Me succulent and fruity.

John Cotton

Pineapple

My face may be rough
        and quite scaly,

And my hair's a bit like
        a punk's,

But inside I'm sweet
        and a bit of a treat,

With ice cream
        and cut up in chunks.

John Cotton

Drink Me!

O o quenches O O O
o o o refreshes o
O o
o o o
O o o O O
o o O
O
O O o o
o O o fizzy O
O o o
o
o o o o
o O o o
O o O
O O
bubbly o o O
O o o o
o o Vitamin C
o o O o o
o
o O
o
O o O o
o O
o O o
o o
guzzling O O o
o
O O
o O o O o o o O
O
Vitamin B_6 O o O
o O
o o O o
o O o Burp! (Pardon me.)

Mike Johnson

Filtered Magic

Turn the coffee maker on

8-cup model, won't take long!

The water rises up until

The next compartment

starts to fill

The coffee's scalded to a frizzle then dribbles down

Just hear it sizzle

Trevor Harvey

Beware the Allivator

The Allivator

at the top.

then eat you

his back

ride upon

let you

he will

in a shop

see one

if you

allivator

Beware the

Roger McGough

The Claw

this is the
shape of the
monster's claw
glinting on its
massive paw
which quietly
opened the
bedroom door
and swung up
with one
terrible roar
over the bed
in the moon-
light before
it stabbed
into the
sleeper
to sil-
ence
his
snor
re
!

blood

d
r
i
p
p
e
d
down on the floor

Dave Calder

Creature

I   am
the   crazy
crater creature,
I creep across the
crater 's   cracks
and cr u nch the
crimson crystals
that cringe in
crooked cul-de-sacs.
Once a crumbling spacecraft crashed—
an ancient cosmonaut crawled clear.
Across the crinkled crust I chased her
and chortling with churlish cheer

caught	the	granny
in	a	cranny
of	the	crater
and	ate	her

Dave Calder

NESSiE rises from the depths of the still lake... and beneath the dark dome of the watching sky the endless ripples circle, lapping from wave to wave...

Judith Nicholls

Corn Circle

WHO TRAMPLED IN THE CORN AND MADE AMAZING PATTERNS OVERNIGHT? IS IT A HOAX, OR DID SOME STRANGE SPACE-CRAFT APPEAR, AND HERE ALIGHT? WHAT WONDERFUL INTELLIGENCE HAS FOUND US OUT, AND LEFT THIS SIGN? AND WILL THEY ONE DAY DARE TO STAY, AND TALK WITH US, AND PROVE BENIGN?

Pam Gidney

53

Save the Smorkle Campaign

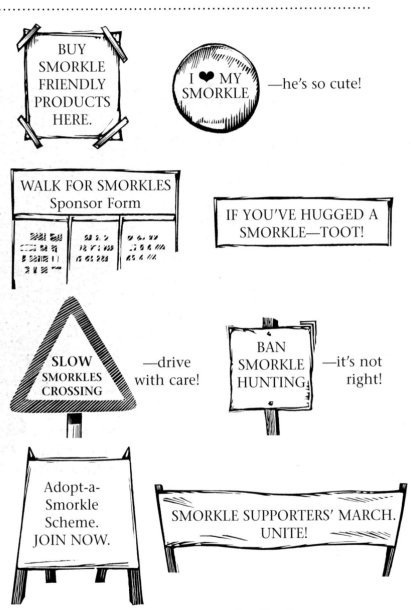

BUY SMORKLE FRIENDLY PRODUCTS HERE.

I ♥ MY SMORKLE —he's so cute!

WALK FOR SMORKLES
Sponsor Form

IF YOU'VE HUGGED A SMORKLE—TOOT!

SLOW SMORKLES CROSSING —drive with care!

BAN SMORKLE HUNTING —it's not right!

Adopt-a-Smorkle Scheme. JOIN NOW.

SMORKLE SUPPORTERS' MARCH. UNITE!

Sue Cowling

The Twenty Steps to the Cellar

You descend with trepidation
one stone step at a time,
your torch illuminating
walls draped with 'webs and grime.
Down this same foot-worn stairway,
for centuries gone by,
tramped scullions and kitchen-maids,
came servants with a sigh
to dump unwanted chattels
by gleam of flick'ring lamp
on the cellar's cold flagstones
amidst the rising damp.
And now their shades surround you,
throng the sour-sweet air,
trailing shrouds of memories
that touch and wisp your hair,
but you must keep descending
a step, then one step more,
until at last you stand upon
the cellar's flagstoned floor.

Wes Magee

For Sale

VICARAGE

Droves
of dry
r o t
creep-
ing up
from the
cellar,
back-biting winds whipping under the door,
Victorian corpse, skin candlewax yellow,
lies on a table-high bed where the floor
tilts like the deck of a ship on an ocean,
creaks as if speaking, glints red in a flicker
of lamplight that wanders in
strange floating motion, held in
the hand of some black-gaitered vicar
who passes through windows
both shuttered and barred, and chanting
winds buckets of blood from a well
that's strangled by yew trees
beside the churchyard.
To view: call the Devil on—666 Hell.

Gina Douthwaite

Hallowe'en Hot-Pot

HALLOWE'EN HOT-POT

Blackhead of a greasy skin
in the cauldron simmering,
hair of nose and wax of ear,
scurf of scalp and salt of tear,
sticky eye and fur of tongue,
plaque of tooth and blood of gum.
For a spell stir at the double,
bring it to the boil
and bubble.

Gina Douthwaite

Word
Smattering

Word Smattering

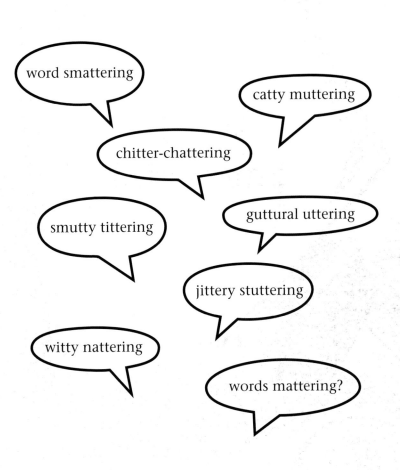

Sue Cowling

Dizzy Dancer's Disco Party starts on Friday, 7.30, at the HITS and MISSES Club, Flip Side, Lyric. Please be good and send your answer promptly back to Dizzy Dancer — R.S.V.P.

R.S.V.P

Dizzy Dancer

45, Stylus, GROOVYTRACK, Charts. TOP20 1CD

Gina Douthwaite

The Letter That Was Never Sent

THE LETTER THAT WAS NEVER SENT

THE FEELINGS THAT YOU

WORDS YOU NEVER SAID

THE SENTIMENTS UNREAD

AND NOW, TOO LATE, ARE HID.

MEANT TO STATE AND NEVER DID THE

Trevor Millum

Soft and **humming** —

LOUD

and **strumming** —

Listen to that NEAT refrain!

Add a **TRUMPET**

And a

DRUM kit—

Why not change the B
E
A
T again?

UP
THE

VOLUME

Eardrum priser,

INSTANT POP GROUP
SyntheSIZER!

Trevor Harvey

I AM THE PHONE THAT
RINGS   AND   RINGS
THE MESSAGE
LEFT UNANSWERED
I AM ALL THE CALLS
HEARD BLEEPING IN AN EMPTY
ROOM LIKE VOICES ENDLESSLY
REPEATING IN A TOMB...

Trevor Millum

Music

```
            l   k
                 c
            e
                 i
            s
                 t
            p
                 s
          e  a
             r
             i
             c
        y    k
        m    l
             e
        d    s
        n         i   c
        u   M u s      t  w
     o          d         s
       r   a    i    t   i
                s
                a
       s        p
        r     p
         a  e
```

David Poulter

Fun and Games

Dive and Dip

Rise and rip, dive and dip, leaning backwards with the strain.
Rattling, roaring, lunging
Looping, lunging,
upward soaring,
swirling whirling in your brain.
downward plunging, going round
a dizzy bend.

Swinging, clinging, heads are ringing, holding tightly to a friend.
Hands that clasp, scream and gasp, funny feelings here inside.
Ears are popping now we're stopping.

That's a roller coaster ride.

Max Fatchen

KickingtheCircleKickingtheCircleKickingtheCircleKickingtheCircleKickingtheCircleKickingtheCircleKickingtheCircleKickingtheCircleKicking

Football

Katherine Gallagher

How to Line Up Your Team

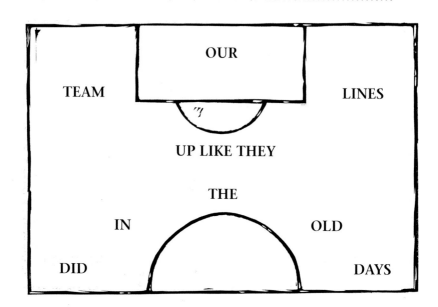

OUR

TEAM   LINES

UP LIKE THEY

THE

IN   OLD

DID   DAYS

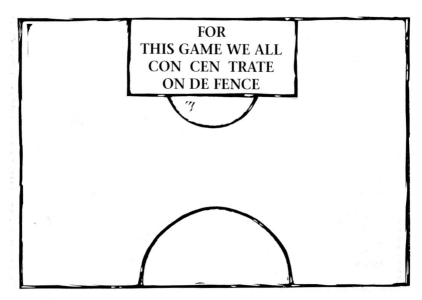

FOR
THIS GAME WE ALL
CON CEN TRATE
ON DE FENCE

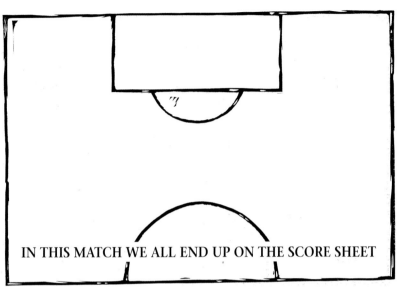

IN THIS MATCH WE ALL END UP ON THE SCORE SHEET

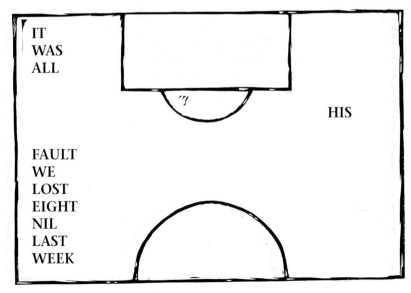

IT
WAS
ALL

HIS

FAULT
WE
LOST
EIGHT
NIL
LAST
WEEK

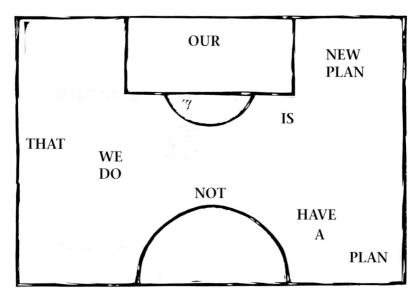

John Coldwell

Duck

Bowler races   Batsman faces
BallBat

F
 i
  e
   l
    d
     e
      r
       c
        h
         a
          s
           e
            s   Howzatt!

Caught
For 0.

John Coldwell

Cricket Bat

DISMAL TEST SCORES {MAKE ME RATTY. I'M A LITTLE {CRICKET BATTY.

Jenny Morris

Such a Racket

Whack- - - - - - crack,
There - - - - and - - - - back,
Whizzing- - - - to and fro.
Swinging- - - swerving,
Sizzling- high - - serving,
Hitting - - - and low.
Lashing- - - crashing,
Dashing- - smashing,
Hear the linesman's call.
Belted- - - - - spun,
There's not much fun,
When you're a tennis ball.

Max Fatchen

Playtime

The thing is not to stand around or lean against the railings looking fed up on your own So what I do is I walk about the playground like I'm dead busy like I'm doing now then just before the whistle blows I've made myself a STAR

David Horner

Only a Game

```
          PRESS - - - Re diddlediddlediddle de de dee...
          GO! Karate Haiku Kid walkwalkwalkwalk
                                              STOP
          Warriors From The Gates Of Dawn     ATTACK
0                       K
                    C  one f        y   y
          UM  I        a         a    a   y
          J P K        I            r  r   a
              . .      I          p  p   r
10         .   s  vanishes in a spray of pixels
                     .  *  .            p p
            P  ./  .              r      r   r
20        one EX   . *        ES          a     a   a
            L . . .              y          y    y

                    *   .  —  .
                           one gets chopped
                                         in ha
30                         lf & disapp....
         Re diddlediddle—BEEP!*BEEP!*BEEP!* – – – a blade  S
                                                            W
                                                             I
                                                       N
                                                    S  G
                         d.g.
              in & Karate Haiku Kid d.o. e.s. OK OK OK walkwalk
40 walkwalkwalkwalk – but
                         WAIT it's the Black HOLE here with
out warning Karate Haiku Kid tries to NRUT but g r a v i t y
p u l l s  him  d o
                   w n
                      .   .
                       .
```

When You Walked Down the Passage

When you walked down the passage what did you see?

A DOOR WITH A MESSAGE THAT I KNEW WAS FOR ME

WHAT DID YOU FIND WHEN YOU OPENED THE DOOR?

I found a wooden chest in the middle of the floor—

what did you find when you opened the lid?

a parcel of paper sealed with wax that was red

what did you find when you op- ened the seal?

a picture of gran dad that was lifelike and real!

what did you see when you looked in his eyes?
a stare that went through me and saw through my lies

Trevor Millum

From Top
        to Toe

Bodies

Bodies are
blood, brains
and bones,
tubes that
loop
and
chromosomes,
organs, gastro-gases, guts, veins and valves,
and glands
with ducts,
fluids, flesh,
fat, feet,
and
fingers,
held in shape
(that's what the
skin does)

so
they
all
look
much
the
same.

That's
why
bodies
need
a
name.

Gina Douthwaite

Riddle Poem

my first is in hair
and also in hat

next   is in
EY   ES
&
also
in nose

my third is in laugh
but not in cries

my last
is   in
beard

but not   in toes

Trevor Millum

79

I
NEED
CONTACT
L E N S E S

like I need a poke in the eye

John Hegley

Who
knows
why a
nose has
hair? Don't
despair for
it's there
to deter
the entry of
dust which
turns to a crust,
clogs nostrils
and blocks off
t
  h   i   r
    e   a

Gina Douthwaite

Belt

Thread me carefully around your waist and fasten me tight or I might let you down. I am a belt.

John Foster

Pants

```
                 the wind came roar
                 ing from the sea
                 it reeled around
                 respectable trees
             it jigged    the roof
             tiles up    and down
          and knoc       ked old
           ladies         to the
          ground          ...but
         worst,          in  its
        rough            panting
       play              it dan
      ced my             clean
      pants               clean
                          away
```

Dave Calder

Shoe

MY FIRST IS IN SOCK BUT NOT IN LOCKING. MY SECOND IN SHOCK BUT NOT IN STOCKING. MY THIRD IS IN BOOT AS WELL AS BROLLY. MY FOURTH IS IN WELLY BUT NOT IN WALLY

Trevor Millum

Steel, Stone,
and Concrete

Pylons

.... PYLONS ....

```
                          P
                          Y
                          L
                          O
                          N
                          S
            tall                    tall
            metal                   steel
            trees                   legs

                    WE TALK

            no                        with
            birds    TO EACH OTHER    firm
            ever       CONSTANTLY     feet
            come                      planted

        MMMMmmmmmmmmMMMM


    nothing    OUR LINES CROSS AND HUM    we
    comes      OUR ARMS OUTSTRETCHED      hum
    near          FINGERS FULL OF         over
    us            L I G H T N I N G       head

MMMMMMmmmmmmmmmmmmmmmmmmmMMMMMMM

    only     WE LINK CITIES AND SEAS TOGETHER    talk
    the          NO CHILDREN WILL PLAY           in
    mist          NEAR US, NO ANIMALS            metal
    comes                                        voices

        WE ARE SHUNNED AND FEARED BY EVERYONE

MMMMMMMmmmmmmmmmmmmmmmmmmmMMMMMMMMM

    slowly     WE HAVE THE POWER TO        stiff
    coils      MAKE THE WORLD GO BLACK     grey
    our        TO CLOSE DOWN THE SYSTEM    strong
    toes           OF THE PLANET EARTH     things
    of power                               of power
    of power                               of power
    of power                               of power
    of power                               of power
MMMMMMMMM                            MMMMMMMMM
```

Christine Morton

Skyscrapers

L
L
A
T
LY
IB
RED
INC
ARE
PERS
SCRA
SKY-
SOME

L
AL
SM
TE
QUI
ARE
SOME

SKY?
THE
PE
RA
SC
TO
ED
NE
WE
DO
WHY
KNOW IS
I WANT TO
BUT WHAT

Tony Langham

The Bridge

Andrew Collett

Pyramid

```
            P
          E A K
        P L A C E
      P R O U D L Y
    P R O V I D I N G
  P R E S T I G I O U S
  P L U S H   P R I V A T E
P I L E D   P E N T H O U S E
P E R F E C T L Y   P L A N N E D
P A N O R A M I C   P O S I T I O N
PART  PAYMENT  POSSIBLE
PAST PHARAOHS PREFERRED
```

Dave Calder

Weekend in the Country

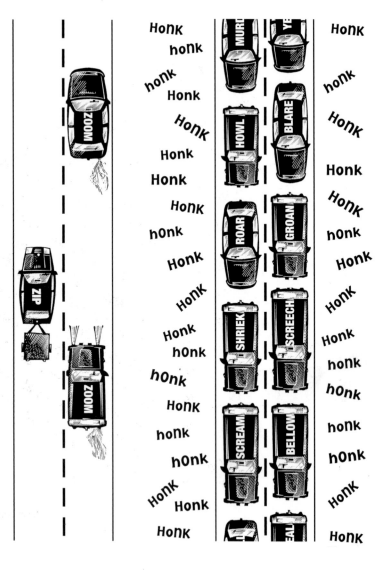

Robert Froman

The Concrete Poem

What is a concrete poem?
It doesn't sound quite right,
For concrete's rather heavy
And words are rather light.

Let's say you write a poem—
'Ode to a concrete slab'—
A subject none too pretty,
Which many would call drab.

Perhaps you could describe it
As full of strength and grace
And muse on what high tower
Might rest upon that base.
You may contrast its texture
With wood and weathered stone
And wonder if it will some day
Be mellowed, creeper-grown.

But if you set the words out
And shape your poem, too,
To be the slab's three faces
With each face seen askew,
So that the poem's reader
Can look as well as hear,
why then, your final poem
Is Concrete—is that clear?

Noel Petty

Index of titles and first lines
First lines are in italic

a thread of light in the darkness 31
Allivator, The 49
Alphabirds 21
Autumn 26

Beech 24
Belt 82
Beware the / allivator 49
Black as a chimney boy 16
Blackbird 19
Blackhead of a greasy skin 57
Blow This 81
Bodies 78
Bodies are 78
Bowler races 71
Breakfast 36
Bridge, The 88
Buy smorkle friendly products here 54

Candy Bar 42
Cat Dream 18
Catherine Wheel 39
Chocolatechocolate 42
Claw, The 50
Clouds 25
Concrete Poem, The 91
Corn Circle 53
Creature 51
Cricket Bat 72

Dismal Test scores 72
Dive and Dip 66
Dizzy Dancer's Disco Party Invitation 60

Dizzy Dancer's Disco Party starts 60
Doggerel 15
Drink Me! 46
Droves of dry rot 56
Duck 71

Eating Out 40

Filtered Magic 47
Fire 27
First the kindling 27
Flies are brave 12
Football 67
Footsteps in the snow 29
For Sale 56
Forks are for twirling spaghetti 43
Frog 14

Ground by cold rolling sea 34

Hallowe'en Hot-Pot 57
Hear the spatter 32
Hippopotamus 13
Holiday Memories 30
horiz n 23
How to Line Up Your Team 68

I am a belt 82
I am a bright round orange 44
I am / the crazy 51
I Am The Phone 64
I am the phone that 64
I Need Contact Lenses 80

I used to go round with her 39

If you sat on a hippo 13

Invasion 20

It was freezing cold 30

Kicking the Circle 67

Lean cuisine 40

Letter That Was Never Sent, The 61

Lion 12

Listen 32

Mined by Moles 16

Mirror ꙅoꙅꙅiM 38

Mouse 18

Music 64

Music twists around my ears 64

My daddy reads at breakfast 36

My face may be rough 45

My first is in hair 79

My first is in sock 84

Nessie 52

Nessie rises from the depths 52

On the wheel of words 8

Only a Game 75

Orange 44

Our team lines up like they 48

Pants 83

Peak place 89

Pineapple 45

Playtime 74

PRESS . . . Re diddlediddle-diddle de de dee . . . 75

Pylons 86

Pyramid 89

quenches 46

Rhythm Machine 62

Riddle Poem 79

Rise and rip, dive and dip 66

Save the Smorkle Campaign 54

Seahorses 33

Sensuous slither 11

Shoe 84

Sisters 37

Skyscrapers 87

Slowly slowly the leaves start to fall 26

Snake's Dance 11

Snowdrop 31

Soft and humming 62

Some skyscrapers are incredibly tall 87

Spaghetti Poem 43

Spider 15

Stone Haiku 34

Such a Racket 73

Sunrise 23

Tall Talk 10

The letter that was never sent 61

The thing is not to stand around or lean 74

The tree-tall giraffe 10

The wind came roar 83

this is the / shape of the 50

trapping flies 15

Trees 24

Turn the coffee maker on 47

Twenty Steps to the Cellar, The 55

Umbrella *25*
Ugly sisters make you wince
14

Waves / and breakers 33
Weekend in the Country
90
Whack . . . crack 73
'What a dog!' means ugly 15
What is a concrete poem? 91
When sky unravels its cold
mysteries 28
When You Walked Down
the Passage 76
When you walked down the
passage what did you see?
76

Who knows why a nose has
hair? 81
Who trampled in the corn 53
Winter 28
Winter Walk 29
With the first edge of light
20
Word Smattering 59
Word Whirls 8

You descend with trepidation
55
You looking out 38
Ys owl 21

Zip Zoom Zoom 90

Index of authors

Benson, Catherine 18, 25
Bowkett, Steve 75
Calder, Dave 11, 21, 50,
51, 83, 89
Coldwell, John 68, 71
Collett, Andrew 88
Cotton, John 44, 45
Cowling, Sue 43, 54, 59
Douthwaite, Gina 16, 19,
37, 56, 57, 60, 78, 81
Edwards, Paula 30
Fatchen, Max 66, 73
Foster, John 8, 82
Froman, Robert 42, 90
Gallagher, Katherine 67
Gidney, Pam 53
Gillilan, Pamela 20
Harrison, Michael 34
Harvey, Trevor 47, 62
Hegley, John 80

Hinn, Helena 31
Holder, Julie 12, 13, 24, 27
Holmes, Maggie 32
Horner, David 39, 74
Johnson, Mike 23, 46
Langham, Tony 26, 87
Leighton, Patricia 29
Lewis, J. Patrick 10, 28, 38
Magee, Wes 55
McGough, Roger 49
Millum, Trevor 15, 61, 64,
76, 79, 84
Morris, Jenny 14, 15, 72
Morton, Christine 86
Nicholls, Judith 40, 52
Petty, Noel 36, 91
Poulter, David 64
Priestley, Janis 33

Acknowledgements

The editor and publisher are grateful for permission to include the following poems:

Catherine Benson: 'Cat Dream' and 'Autumn', both Copyright © Catherine Benson 1998, first published in this collection by permission of the author. **Steve Bowkett**: 'Only a Game', first published in Trevor Harvey (ed.): *Techno Talk (poems with byte)* (Bodley Head, 1994), reprinted by permission of the author. **Dave Calder**: 'Snake's Dance' from *Bamboozled* (Other Publications, 1987); 'Alphabirds', 'The Claw', 'Creature', 'Pants', and 'Pyramid', all Copyright © Dave Calder 1998, first published in this collection, all by permission of the author. **John Coldwell**: 'How to Line Up Your Team' first published in David Orme (ed.): *You'll Never Walk Alone* (Macmillan, 1995); 'Duck', Copyright © John Coldwell 1998, first published in this collection, both by permission of the author. **Andrew Collett**: 'The Bridge', Copyright © Andrew Collett 1998, first published in this collection by permission of the author. **John Cotton**: 'Orange' and 'Pineapple', both Copyright © John Cotton 1998, first published in this collection by permission of the author. **Sue Cowling**: 'Spaghetti Poem', 'Save the Smorkle Campaign', and 'Word Smattering', all Copyright © Sue Cowling 1998, first published in this collection by permission of the author. **Gina Douthwaite**: 'Sisters' and 'Dizzy Dancer's Disco Party Invitation' from *Picture a Poem* (Hutchinson, 1994), Copyright © Gina Douthwaite 1994; 'Blow This', first published in *Nothing Tastes Quite Like a Gerbil* (Macmillan, 1996), Copyright © Gina Douthwaite 1996, 'Mined by Moles', 'Blackbird', 'For Sale', 'Hallowe'en Hot-Pot', and 'Bodies', all Copyright © Gina Douthwaite 1998, first published in this collection, all by permission of the author. **Paula Edwards**: 'Holiday Memories', first published in Gervase Phinn (ed.): *Lizard Over Ice* (Nelson), reprinted by permission of Gervase Phinn. **Max Fatchen**: 'Dive and Dip' and 'Such a Racket', from *Peculiar Rhymes and Lunatic Lines* (first published in the UK by Orchard Books, a division of the Watts Publishing Group, 96 Leonard Street, London EC2A 4RH, reprinted by permission of the publishers. **John Foster**: 'Word Whirls' and 'Belt', Copyright © John Foster 1998, first published in this collection by permission of the author. **Robert Froman**: 'Candy Bar' (originally entitled 'Well, Yes') from *Street Poems* (McCall Pub. Co., 1971) and 'A Weekend in the Country' from *Seeing Things* (T. Crowell, 1974), reprinted by permission of Katherine Froman. **Katherine Gallagher**: 'Football', Copyright © Katherine Gallagher 1998, first published in this collection by permission of the author. **Pam Gidney**: 'Corn Circle', Copyright © Pam Gidney 1998, first published in this collection by permission of the author. **Pamela Gillilan**: 'Invasion', first published in John Foster (ed.) *A Fifth Poetry Book* (OUP, 1985), Copyright © Pamela Gillilan 1985, reprinted by permission of the author. **Michael Harrison**: 'Stone Haiku' from *Junk Mail* (OUP, 1993), reprinted by permission of the author. **Trevor**